The — WRITING *Process*

A Step-by-Step Approach for Everyday Writers

DAVID HATCHER AND LANE GODDARD

Landa Books

1873 Meadowbrook Drive, Winston-Salem, North Carolina 27104
www.landabooks.com

ISBN 0-9729920-2-2

LandaBooks
1873 Meadowbrook Drive
Winston-Salem, North Carolina 27104
Voice: (336) 354 8238
Fax: (480) 247 5750
info@LandaBooks.com
http://www.LandaBooks.com

Cover design by Shelley Kirby, Dallas, Texas

—— FOREWORD ——

Writing isn't just finding words to express thoughts. It's also organizing thoughts so they can be put into words.

Some people say that writing is a personal, individual act and can't be taught. It's true that you don't (and won't) write exactly the way anyone else does. But it's also true that almost all good writers use some sort of step-by-step process they've developed and adapted to their own needs.

The goal of this book is to describe one proven way to break your writing tasks into a series of logical steps that will help you get from idea (or assignment) to finished product. Once you've learned the process, you may find that you can sometimes skip a step, or change the order. But you'll probably keep coming back to the process, and choosing the steps that fit your specific project.

Writing is hard work. We can't promise that you'll write effortlessly using this process, but you'll write with less *wasted* effort. It works for us, it works for our students, and we think it will work for you.

CONTENTS

—— WHAT IS ——
"GOOD WRITING"

Good writing is like lots of other intangibles, like beauty or art — we can't define it, but we think we know it when we see it.

Even if we can't come up with a precise definition, we can identify some of the essential elements of good writing.

The Three C's

Good writing is clear, it is concise, it is correct.

This doesn't mean that our writing will be great if it has all three of these qualities. It does mean that it *cannot* be great, or even good, if it does not have them all. So let's take a look at each.

It's Clear

What is clear writing? A good working definition is that it's writing that your intended reader can understand in one reading.

That sounds simple, but lots of writing fails this test. Too many writers feel that if their writing is clear to them, it will be clear to others.

If a word or sentence has two possible interpretations, the writer will know which is intended. But the reader doesn't have this advantage, and may see it the other way.

So what can you do to make sure your writing is clear? Here are two suggestions.

First, you should ask someone else to read your draft. (This is a suggestion we'll revisit often.) It's impossible for the writer, who knows the intent, who's been working and reworking the sentences, to see them as a new reader would. So get some fresh eyes — another competent person to give you a different perspective.

Here's a good rule for people who write for distribution outside the office: Nothing goes out until it has been read by at least one person other than the writer. For important stuff, make that at least two other people.

Second, all writers, editors, and proofers should remember that it's not enough to write so that you can be understood; you must write so that you *can not be misunderstood.* It's sort of a Murphy's Law for writers, and it can prevent lots of grief.

Any good grammar course will cover specific usage points that often cause misunderstanding. But most writers already know how to fix these problems, once they see them. Even if they aren't sure about the cause, they can revise until the meaning is clear.

So a skeptical eye is more important than knowledge of grammar rules. Look hard for any word or sentence that could possibly be misinterpreted, and do what's needed to fix it.

It's Concise

"Concise writing," according to writing teacher Walt Skretch, "means saying the same thing — *once*."

Many groups — educators, lawyers, government employees — have been accused of producing writing that is intended to impress rather than to express.

It's easy to pretend that only other people produce fat writing. The truth is that almost all writers, including experienced professionals, often write wordy first drafts.

But many of these professionals find that it's more effective to keep up the momentum of writing, to plunge on through to the end, and then to come back later and begin the job of trimming down.

Sure, you can learn to write more concisely from the beginning. But don't get the idea that your first drafts are ready to be shipped out the door to the waiting public. This just doesn't happen, even to professionals.

For anything more complex than a note to your kids or a co-worker, make sure you go back over it to trim extra words. Or better still, let a good editor do it.

It's Correct

When we say that our writing must be "correct," we usually mean that it must be reasonably free of errors in grammar, punctuation, spelling, and word usage. That's not a bad working definition. But it might help if we also take a look at what we *don't* mean by the word.

One of the most widespread ideas is that somewhere out there is an authority that can answer all our usage questions. There isn't. Our language is constantly changing, and what's acceptable at one time and place is unacceptable in another.

Good writers know that many words have variant spellings, pronunciations, and definitions — all acceptable. They know that Shakespeare spelled his own name different ways, that early editors would choose a spelling to fit the space available, and that *ain't* was perfectly acceptable for many years.

All that said, we still have to produce writing that conforms to some standard of acceptability. In most of our work-related writing, we use "formal standard English," with rules that are:

- Based on the written language of established writers
- Codified in English grammar texts
- Taught in schools
- Reinforced by editors, teachers, and writers

Suggestions for Correctness

Here are a few specific suggestions, boiled down to what has proved most helpful to writers we've known:

- Decide which style manual your group or office will use
- Recognize that it won't answer all your questions
- If you need to, start your own style sheet (for yourself or your work group)
- If possible, designate a "decider" for arguable questions
- Be open to reasonable exceptions to the rules
- Change the rules when you need to

—— THE WRITING —— PROCESS

We're All Different

No two people speak or write exactly the same way. Your personal pattern (called your *idiolect*) is also unique — nobody else knows or uses precisely the same words you do, or uses them in the same way. Every skilled and successful writer has developed a style that is unlike anyone else's.

But most successful writers do have some things in common. One of the most important is that they've learned to take their writing through a process — a series of steps — that they know will get them from the idea stage through to the finished written product.

They don't all use the same process, of course. But there is a lot of commonality, and the one we describe here combines the steps that many good writers follow.

All these steps are important. If you learn and follow them, your writing *will* improve. We strongly recommend that you work through them all, making sure you understand the importance of each one. Later, you can vary the steps, tailoring them to fit the specific needs of your immediate writing task.

Let's start by looking at the whole process, then we'll focus on each step.

Steps in the Writing Process

- **Step One:** Establish Your Purpose and Identify Your Reader
- **Step Two:** Get Organized
- **Step Three:** Write a First Draft
- **Step Four:** Age the Draft
- **Step Five:** Reread the Draft
- **Step Six:** Revise
- **Step Seven:** Edit
- **Step Eight:** Proofread

Step One: Establish Your Purpose and Identify Your Reader

This step sounds so basic that you may think it's not necessary to mention it. But it's one of the most important of these steps, and it's very often overlooked.

People too often identify only the topic, then jump right in and begin writing without giving much thought to their readers or their purpose. But without a clear understanding of both, it's hard to produce good writing.

Here's what H.J. Tichy, a respected writing teacher, has to say:

> *A clearly established statement of purpose is the most important single requirement for effective technical writing. You simply can't make sure you've done something well unless you know what it was you intended to do.*

So start by thinking hard about who is going to read your piece, and what you want it to accomplish. Then write a short and simple statement of your purpose. Reread and revise it until it clearly says what you want it to say.

Step Two: Get Organized

The writing process can be boiled down to two steps.

- Planning and organizing
- Writing and rewriting

What most people fail to realize is that the first step is at least as important as the second. Over the years we've found that the majority of writing problems (our own as well as our students') can be traced back to inadequate planning and organizing.

So a plan, an organized structure or skeleton, is essential to good, clear writing. And your plan must be developed with two things in mind: what your purpose is, and who your readers are.

This does not mean that your plan must be long and complex. In fact, you don't always have to make a formal outline before you begin your draft. Sometimes you will need to do only two things in this planning and organizing stage.

Two Essentials

At a minimum, you should make a carefully thought-out list of the points needed to achieve your purpose, and put these points in some kind of logical order.

Next, ask yourself if you have the information and resources you need to make those points. If not, make filling those gaps part of your plan.

When you're taking on a more challenging writing job, you'll need to match both the writing plan and the organization to the complexity of your task. The next section will give you some information on different ways to organize, so you can match your structure to your material and purpose.

Step Three: Write a First Draft

Writing that first draft is one of your most important steps. It's also one of the least understood, so it's often done poorly.

People usually have trouble with their drafts for one of two reasons: They undervalue it, or they overvalue it.

The attitude of those who undervalue it is something like "Oh, it's only a draft. It's important to get something down on paper, so I'll jump right in and sorta think through my fingers. I'll just put down whatever thoughts come to me, in the order they occur."

Write a Draft, Not a Drift

That's like the wind blowing snowflakes around — and with the same results. The formless thing you end up with is a drift, not a draft. If you haven't followed some plan in writing your draft, you'll probably be in worse shape than before you started. You now have to undo the mess, which is often harder than starting over.

Writers who overvalue the draft seem to think "This piece of writing is *me* — and it's got to be good." That's not always a bad attitude — as far as the final product is concerned. But one benefit of the draft is that it lets us build a skeleton that's roughly in the planned shape of the final product, without having to worry (yet) about all the little details.

Right the First Time?

Approaching the draft with the attitude of "I've gotta do it right the first time" is like trying to carve a statue by starting at the top of a block of stone and working only once to the bottom, ending up with a finished product. It makes much more sense to carve the block into roughly the shape you want, and then to go back over it, making finer adjustments each time.

So after you've organized your points, go ahead and start your draft. (Your statement of purpose can be a good start.) Then, without agonizing or straining, write down what you want to say about your first point.

You don't have to finish the entire draft at one sitting. If it's short (a letter or memo), of course you can plunge on through.

You'll almost certainly find it more productive to break longer projects into smaller chunks — such as chapters or sections — that you can finish drafting without tiring yourself out, or losing concentration. Keep up your momentum by planning — and following — a schedule for finishing the entire draft.

Don't Expect Perfection

Don't expect the draft to be perfect, and don't stop to edit yourself or worry about details at this stage. That'll come later.

If you follow your plan without getting bogged down in premature editing, you'll end up with a good draft.

The sentences may not sing, but you'll have a piece of work that's organized and follows your plan.

Step Four: Age That First Draft

Aging the draft means letting go of it, putting it away and forgetting about it for a while — preferably overnight, at least.

You may say you don't have time. But that's almost never a valid excuse. This step is not a trivial point or a nicety. Make the time to put that draft away — let it ripen and mellow a little. You may be surprised at how much it changes.

Step Five: Reread Your Draft

After you've aged your draft, read it from beginning to end. Resist that urge to tinker as you read. Your main purpose is to evaluate the overall structure — to check on the organization.

It's okay to make tick marks or quickly circle things you want to come back to, but don't stop to fiddle around with details now.

Step Six: Revise (But Don't Edit)

This step involves big changes only. Don't worry about spelling, punctuation, or niceties of word choice.

There are three reasons for avoiding the temptation to tinker with the tiny things.

First, it's a waste of time. You're almost certain to throw out some of the sentences you revise, so why polish them first?

Second, it can be frustrating. After you fuss and fiddle with the minor points, you'll find that the big problems are still there.

Third, you may fall in love with the draft as it is. The more you fool around with the sentences — changing a word here, moving a comma there — the more they become your children, your babies. And the more reluctant you become to make the big changes that are really needed. So make the major changes first, and save the little ones for later.

Do

- Move or delete whole segments that are in the wrong place or are unnecessary to your purpose.
- Mark any places where you've omitted something important, or where you need to expand or support a point.

Step Seven: Edit

At this stage, you can fine-tune, fiddle a little with the details. Now you're working on things like sentence structure, word choice, grammar, spelling, and punctuation.

Because it's detailed work, and because you've already been toiling over the sentences, the job can get tedious. If you get too tired of it, you're increasing the risk that you'll overlook something that needs changing. This is a place in the writing process where you should try to find someone else — someone whose judgment you respect — to read and comment on your writing.

Get Honest Help

This is a bit tricky. You ask for criticism, but underneath you want your readers to say good things about your writing. If they're your friends, and if you let them, they'll probably say good things about it.

Don't let them.

Make a Deal

Tell them at the beginning that you want and need their frank and honest suggestions. And don't make them feel they have to justify what they say. You might make an agreement with them. They'll be free to say anything at all about your writing, and you'll simply say thanks. You won't argue or explain why you wrote it the way you did, why they're wrong, and why you really shouldn't change it.

And the other part of the deal is that you'll be just as free to accept or ignore their suggestions. But of course you'll give them careful consideration, otherwise why ask?

Be sure to say thanks, at least. Your readers are doing you a big favor.

Step Eight: Proofread

No matter how hard you've worked on it, your writing will need a careful rereading to weed out typos, and to make sure punctuation, grammar, word choice, and spelling follow standard usage rules.

Don't try to do this yourself. It's almost impossible to correct your own work. If your writing is to be nearly error free, another pair of sharp eyes is essential. (It's better if the proofer hasn't seen the earlier drafts.) If you can find others you work well with, you can form a good mutual-aid team. You read their stuff, and they read yours.

And **don't** depend on your spellchecker. It will let you down.

Summary

That's one approach to the writing process, and it's a proven one. If you want to (or have to) use another, that's okay. But be sure you have a systematic process, and follow it as closely as you can.

"Oh, I only write letters," you say. "I can't go through all this every time I have to write a simple letter." *Yes, you can.* You might adapt the process, perhaps by jotting your purpose and main points, drafting the letter (or email), letting it rest while you get a cup of coffee or go to lunch — you get the picture.

Here are a few more suggestions, based on comments from successful writers.

- **Schedule a time and place for your writing.** Like Pavlov's dog, we find that our juices flow better when we have associations going on — like writing at a regular time and in the same place.

- **Don't go snowblind.** Don't freeze up and begin staring at the white page (or blank screen). Get something down, following your plan.

- **Work hard on your opening and closing paragraphs.** Just as the first and final sentences of a paragraph are the most important, so are the first and final paragraphs of the whole work.

If you follow an orderly process, your writing will improve. You'll enjoy it more (or dislike it less), and what's more important — your readers will understand and enjoy it too.

Now that you've had an overview of the whole writing process, let's take a closer look at each step.

——A FEW WORDS ——
ABOUT YOUR PURPOSE

Every time you write, you should have a specific goal in mind.

Most of us, when we sit down to begin a writing task, have a fairly clear idea of the *topic* or *message* we want to get across, and have given time and thought to any facts and figures we want to include. But a common danger is to focus too narrowly on the specific content of the message, and to neglect two critically important factors: the *purpose* of our writing, and our *intended readers.*

On different days, in different writing projects, you may write for a variety of reasons — such as to persuade, inform, entertain, or instruct. You may want to make a request, and need to support your case for having it granted. Maybe you need to explain your position on an issue, or want to refute someone else's position (as when you write a letter to the editor countering an article or editorial). You may want to apply for a job, submit an article for publication, or suggest a change in the way an organization operates.

A Change in the Reader

Each of these goals asks your reader to make a change, even if only to consider a new idea or approach. If your writing brings about this change, it has succeeded. If it doesn't, it has failed — even if it is clear and organized, gets right to the point, states that point clearly, and supports the point.

If you keep your purpose and readers in mind from the beginning — from the planning and organizing all the way through to final proofreading — you are much more likely to organize your points, structure your sentences, and choose your words in a way that will help you reach your goal.

A Few Purposes to Consider

Here are a few sample purposes for writing. Of course there are others, but these should help you consider some of the ways that your purpose affects all aspects of your writing.

To Inform: This is a common purpose of work-related and academic writing. The goal is to give your readers new information — to explain how to use a piece of equipment, to announce a change in budget or schedule, to lay out a plan for a project, to define a term.

To Answer a Question: A good deal of work-related and academic writing also involves answering questions. These Q-and-A exchanges may be informal (a short, penned note from your supervisor with your reply added on the same page, or your emailed answer to a phone call) or formal (an answer to an exam question, or to a client's query).

Two important points about your replies: be sure you answer the question clearly, and that you avoid the common fault of providing too much information. And when you can, reply promptly — especially if there's a note of urgency in the request, or (consider your reader) if it's your supervisor or someone else you think deserves a little special consideration. Of course you'll sometimes add a little extra information, when you think it's needed. But as a rule, keep your answers short, factual, and prompt.

To Request: Another common purpose for writing is to ask for something, such as information, approval, assistance, or funding. Remember that the person who's going to decide (your reader) may consider only your written words in making the decision, and may already have a position or inclination toward an answer. If you keep such factors in mind as you write, you're more likely to get approval.

To Persuade: When writing to persuade, your aim is to convince your readers to do something, to believe something, to change an attitude. Types of writing that routinely include persuasion as a major goal include advertising, political writing, editorials, and newspaper columns. But we often need to use persuasion in our everyday writing. We aim for persuasion when we request approval or assistance (as above), and when we propose a new procedure, or advocate a change to existing rules or processes.

To Dissuade: When you write to *persuade*, you are trying to get your readers to adopt a new position, often on something they haven't already made up their minds about, or maybe haven't even heard of. In *dissuasion*, you know that your readers already have a position, and your goal is to change their minds — to convince them to give up a present belief or attitude, and to adopt the one you are advocating.

If you combine dissuasion with persuasion (as often happens), your three-part job is to point out disadvantages of the old, to contrast these with advantages of the new, and to show your readers why the sum of the differences makes your idea a better one.

To Sell or Promote Something — Like Yourself:
"Sell" doesn't always mean convincing someone to pay money for goods or services. You may be selling an idea, a suggestion, or yourself (when you apply for a job).

You begin by sifting through the facts and deciding which ones to present, in what order. Putting the most important or most applicable one first is usually a good idea, but not always. You may decide to go in chronological order, if that promises to work best.

You'll *consider* whether or not to address anything that might be considered negative by your reader, and decide which information to put in writing and which to save for an interview or other face-to-face meeting.

Other Possible Purposes

You might also write to interest or entertain, to educate or train, to enlighten, reinforce, reassure, keep in touch, recruit, follow up, document or create a record.

Whatever word you choose to describe it, be sure that you can state your purpose in one sentence. Only then are you ready to move to the next step in writing: getting organized.

— THE WHOLE WORK — GETTING ORGANIZED

Kinds of Organization

Many writing books say that organization is one of the keys to good writing. That's true. Yet there are as many ways to organize what you write as there are possible combinations of your points. How do you choose?

Although you could invent your own structure, you'll probably use one (or a combination) of the most common patterns. After all, they're common because they've proven to be the most useful. So learn them, and use them whenever they're appropriate. But don't feel that you are locked into any of them.

Remember this when considering what structure to use: The reason we care about organization is that it's essential to getting our message across. Choose the structure that best matches your purpose.

Now let's look at some of the most common ways to organize.

Starting With Your Main Point (Order of Importance)

And we're starting with order of importance because it's *our* main point — it's one of the best ways to structure your writing. If you get to the main point right away, you make your job and the reader's job much easier. And your writing is much more likely to work — to get your message across to the reader before a lot of other information gets in the way.

The writer who withholds the main message is in danger of losing the reader, who'll start to ask "What is this paper getting at?" When that happens, you've created a deficit that's hard to recover from.

You can follow up with the other points you think the reader will need. You can clarify, explain, support, provide additional details. Your reader, who already has the main point in mind, will have something to relate this other information to.

So remember — whenever you think it'll work, put your main point up front.

Inventory and Explanation

Here you follow the old preacher's advice: First you tell them what you're going to tell them, and then you tell them what you told them you'd tell them.

Here's an example of an opening inventory paragraph: *There are three steps in refinishing furniture: (1) removing the old finish, (2) preparing the wood, and (3) applying new finish.* Following paragraphs would deal with each of the steps, and a concluding paragraph might summarize, or comment on the pleasure of having completed the job.

This structure is useful when you have several points of near-equal importance. Suppose you want to present four criteria that will be used (and given equal weight) in evaluating applicants for a job, or proposals for a contract.

You'd open by listing the criteria (the inventory of points you plan to cover), and telling the reader that each would be explained in the paragraphs to follow.

Then you'd take the points (criteria) one at a time, explaining each in enough detail to prepare the reader to apply (or bid).

Cause and Effect

This method of organizing is useful when you want to explain the relationship between an action (or event) and its result.

Recommendation and Justification

For example, you may want to recommend an action (maybe the hiring of another person), and you justify your recommendation by outlining the specific result (benefits). You'd probably begin with your recommendation (the purpose of your letter or memo), and then move on to the benefits.

So you'd also be putting your main point first. (See why it's a little artificial to say there are only X number of ways to organize? We're combining at least two here.) And you could end with a restatement of the request, with specific details. (Example: *If you approve, please sign the attached personnel-action form for an entry-level data analyst.*)

Problem and Source

This cause-and-effect structure would also work when you want to provide information on an existing problem (e.g., an increase in error rate), and to identify the source of the problem (such as inadequate training on new software).

You could begin by briefly stating the problem (which is the *effect* of inadequate training), and then tell what you believe to be the source (i.e., the *cause*) of the problem. It's quite likely that you'd also recommend some action (maybe a training course), so you'd be stringing together three elements: effect (errors), cause (untrained people), and a recommended action (training) to eliminate the problem.

So you see that cause-and-effect writing can work backward or forward, and in different combinations and orders. It can be an excellent way to get your points across to the reader, in the order you want them. But be careful to keep things as simple as possible, because if you move back and forth among the points too often, your readers may lose track of where you're leading them.

Order of Time (Chronological Order)

Time order is used in reporting something that has happened, or outlining events in a plan. It can be an effective way to inform readers about a series of actions that they must take.

If your organization is planning a big project that involves new offices, new equipment, new procedures, new training, and new products, somebody had better inform people — early and often — about the necessary actions, who's responsible for each, and the time order in which they must occur.

Spatial

Not used as often as the others, spatial (also spelled *spacial*) order is needed when you want to describe a physical structure or layout.

When would you use it? In giving instructions for assembling something, in describing the floor plan of a building, or in giving directions to a meeting site.

Poor directions will almost guarantee strained relations — they're frustrating. So when you use this order, ask someone who'll be frank with you to play the devil's advocate. Have the person read over your draft as carefully and critically as possible, trying to find any flaws (before your intended readers do).

If you're giving directions for doing something (installing software, putting a toy together), one of the best ways to make sure you accomplish your purpose is to have someone (with equal or less experience than your intended reader) actually follow the directions. If there are problems, you can rewrite to take care of them.

Summary

We've looked at a few of the most common and useful ways to organize our writing. It's helpful to know them.

But the most important thing to remember in planning your own structure is that you want it to be the organization that will best accomplish your purpose. You want it to *work*. So after you've written your purpose statement and listed your points, there are a couple of things you should ask yourself.

Two Questions

First, what do you want your readers to *know* or *do* after reading? Second, what's the best way to organize your points to make this clear to your readers? You want them not only to understand each point, but also to see the relationship between points.

These questions, and your answers to them, can mean the difference between the success and failure of your writing. Remember — lack of organization is the most common writing problem. And skill at organizing (which comes from practice and willingness to work) is a key difference between those people whose writing works and those whose writing doesn't work.

On the next page is an example of a simple but effective approach to planning and organizing.

Here are a couple of questions for you to consider as you look at it: If you were the writer, is there anything you would *not* put in writing? If so, would you communicate any of your omissions? How?

Sample Organization Plan

Purpose: *To get approval for increased funding for my project*

Reader: *Person within agency with authority to approve transfer of funds*

Points Listed	Points Ordered
Agency has $$, I can identify *Proj took hit last yr* *Morale low — attrition* *Create new jobs* *Benefits/results of approval* *-More profs on staff (my promo?)* *-imprvmnts in mission* *Criticism (PAC, media, locals)* *New law (last yr) mandates expansion. We're delinquent. Congr. comm may investigate* *States involved need help*	*Purpose: To request approval of urgently needed funds to accomplish project mission.* *Background: New law mandates this; we're delinquent because underfunded, understaffed; Congressional committee asking questions, with more coming.* *Justification:* *Needs — States in trouble* *Benefits:* *Comply with law; improve staff professionalism; Goodwill with Congr., public* *How we'll spend $/Benefits:* *[Where funds come from? Include?] Talk w/ BERT (lunch)* *Summary, volunteer to brief, answer questions*

— YOUR PARAGRAPHS — WHAT ARE THEY FOR?

Now that you've finished steps one and two, you're ready for step three — writing the first draft. For shorter projects, this usually means writing a paragraph about each of your points.

But just exactly what is a paragraph? What is it supposed to do for you and the reader? Let's take a quick look at the etymology of the word, which is built from two common Greek roots. The first, *para*, means beside. The second, *graph*, means write.

A long time ago, writers simply started at the top of the page and filled up all the lines, all the way across. They rarely, if ever, used indentions or blank lines. This saved on expensive paper (or papyrus or parchment), but made it hard for the reader to see where one topic ended and another began.

Topic Shifts

Then one day some clever wordsmith came up with a helpful idea — why not put some kind of mark to show the reader where the breaks between topics were?

Like many good ideas, this one caught on big. One mark often used was a symbol much like the Greek letter Pi (Π). It was written in the margin, beside the last line of the topic. That's why it was called a paragraph — the mark was placed *beside* the *writing*.

Later the mark was put on a line by itself, near the center of the page. This created a nearly blank line between topics, making it still easier for the reader to see the writer's intended structure. And it also made the mark itself unnecessary, because the blank line would show the division between topics. So the mark was eventually dropped, and a block of writing between blank lines came to be called a paragraph. (Editors still use the mark to show where the text should be split to form an additional paragraph.)

Reader's Guideposts

So a major reason for dividing our writing into paragraphs is to show the reader our intended structure. Skillful paragraphing can help lead the reader through the logical process that you, the writer, have imposed on your information. But this can happen only if you have a logical structure in mind before you start writing. Now let's get a little more specific about how you can write better paragraphs.

Fleshing Out Your Outline

A Quick Recap

Whether you make a detailed outline or not, one of your first steps in writing should be to list your most important points. For a memo or simple letter, that list may be all the outline you need. The usual relationship between the outline (or list) and the first draft is this: each major point should become a separate paragraph. That's a common and efficient way to do a first draft — by thinking about each point and developing it into its own paragraph.

There will be exceptions, of course. Sometimes you can combine two points into one paragraph, and sometimes you'll want to devote more than one paragraph to a point. But if you want to keep your draft clear, simple, and effective, stick as close to the rule as you can.

An Example: The Meeting Site

Suppose you've been asked (or volunteered) to look into the options for a place to hold an upcoming important meeting. You've checked prices, transportation, availability and such, and you've made a short list of acceptable places. Now you want to write up your findings. Each possibility on your list might become a separate paragraph.

The Three-Piece Suit

One of the simplest and most effective writing structures for a job like this is a variation of the inventory-and-explanation structure. It's sometimes called the three-piece suit. The first piece (usually the opening paragraph) tells the readers what you're going to tell them — it explicitly lists the points you intend to make. It might look something like this:

> My purpose is to provide information on three sites that I believe are acceptable for the division meeting: Hotel A, Government Facility B, and Convention Center C. I will summarize pertinent information about each, and will then recommend one of these sites.

The second piece (often several subpieces) is a series of paragraphs dealing with your points, usually one paragraph for each point. So in this example, the second paragraph would deal with the hotel, the third with the government facility, and the fourth with the center.

The third piece (which will probably be the last paragraph) is your ending. It would contain a recommendation, perhaps with a brief statement of justification as a zinger to strengthen your close.

Clean and Simple

The advantages of this structure include clarity and simplicity — it's very easy for the reader to follow. If your subject is more complex, then of course you would be unable to deal with each major point in only one paragraph (because each major point would include a subgroup of subordinate points — and each subordinate point would become a paragraph). But the principle still applies — a paragraph should be a logical subunit, a chewable mental bite, presented to your reader as part of a logical sequence.

Another Example: The Reorganization

You've been asked to do some research on ways to reorganize your division to increase effectiveness. Your research points to three reasonable possibilities, and your judgment tilts you toward one of these. If you choose to follow the three-piece-suit structure in writing your report, your opening could look something like this:

> My purpose is to present three options for reorganizing our division: a matrix structure, a project-management organization, and a combination of the two. I will briefly describe each (with advantages and disadvantages), and will recommend the one that appears most practical.

Because your subject is more complex and your data more extensive, you will need more than one paragraph for each subtopic. You will probably devote a section of several pages to each option, and end with your recommendation and conclusion. The structure will work, provided that you guide the reader with typographical aids (boldface type, subheads, etc.) and stick to the process, presenting information in the order you've promised the reader.

Writing Paragraphs

Some books define a paragraph as a group of sentences dealing with one topic. That's not a perfect definition, but it fits most paragraphs — they're groups of sentences related to a main point.

Let's summarize. You've listed your points, then put them into some kind of order. You've stated each point in the form of a sentence, and now you want to build on these sentences, often using each one as the nucleus, or topic sentence, of a separate paragraph. The other sentences in each paragraph support the topic sentence in some way — they explain, justify, elaborate, or clarify — or they make a smooth transition to the next paragraph.

Where to Put the Topic Sentence

One of the writer's most important jobs is to make the reader's job as easy as possible. You might think that the reader's job will be easiest if you always put the topic sentence first. But don't. Vary the placement of topic sentences.

Two Reasons

For one thing, readers tend to get bored with too much of the same thing. To avoid a repetitive style, you should put topic sentences in different places — not just to keep the reader interested, but also to help your writing make points in different ways.

Another reason is effectiveness. There are times when you'll do a better job of making your point if you put the topic sentence somewhere other than at the beginning. If you are giving the reader some bad news, or expressing an opinion that your reader is unlikely to agree with, you may want a few lead-in sentences to soften the blow, or to make acceptance more likely. Sure, we like writing that gets right to the point — it's almost always better. But not always, so keep your options open, and put the topic sentence where you think it will do the best job.

Kinds of Paragraphs

How can you decide where the topic sentence should go to best fit the purpose of the paragraph? Although every situation is different, here are some common paragraph-structure patterns to consider. One convenient way to describe them is by shape: the widest part of the shape shows where the central thought (or topic sentence) is.

The Straight-News Paragraph (or "Inverted Pyramid")

A straight-news paragraph opens with the topic sentence and then supports it in the following sentences. Here's an example:

> The Smythe Conference Center is the best place for our annual meeting. It is located near a Metro stop, which means that all attendees will be able to reach it without worrying about parking. The meeting rooms are big enough for the number of people we expect, and all have movable partitions for subdividing into breakout rooms. Food is available (there's a good cafeteria), and (perhaps most important) the price is well within our budget.

The Pyramid Paragraph

Sometimes you'll want to save the main point, putting it last. This means writing what is sometimes called a pyramid paragraph. Here's one.

> Because several people have expressed strong opinions about the importance of selecting a good site for the annual meeting, we rated all the reasonable choices by first identifying key factors, and then used these factors in rating each site. These factors included location, price, accessibility, availability of food, size of meeting rooms, and amenities (such as pool, sauna, exercise room). Our preliminary assessment was reviewed by representatives of every division, who unanimously agreed with our recommendation. Accordingly, we have

selected the Smythe Conference Center as the site for our annual meeting.

The Block Paragraph

Sometimes the writer's job is to provide information and let the reader draw a conclusion. When this is the case, you should consider the block paragraph, which does not explicitly state a main point or conclusion.

> As requested, the committee has collected information on the three sites being considered for our meeting, and has given each site a numerical rating (10=excellent, down to 1=barely adequate) on total cost (C), facilities (F), and location (L). The conference center ratings are C-8, F-9, and L-7. The departmental auditorium ratings are C-10, F-4, and L-8. The Azalea Inn ratings are C-8, F-6, and L-7. Details are found in the enclosed chart.

The Diamond Paragraph

As the name suggests, the main point is near the middle of the diamond paragraph. Here's one example:

> Because the meeting site is an important (and somewhat emotional) issue for many of our members, the committee carefully evaluated each possible site in regard to price, location, and quality of meeting facilities. Our conclusion is that the Smythe Conference Center is the best choice. The price is within our budget (in fact, we'll have $5,000 left as a contingency fund). The location is reasonably convenient (it's just outside the beltway, very near a Metro station).

Most important, the meeting facilities are excellent for our needs, with plenty of space, six breakout rooms, and good audiovisual equipment.

Summary

We've looked at the development of a writing task from concept through major points to paragraphs. We've considered a few of the most common ways to construct paragraphs around the major point (which is usually expressed in a topic sentence). Now we're ready to look at ways to evaluate paragraphs you've drafted.

What Makes a Paragraph Effective — Or Ineffective?

After you've completed your first draft, and before you start worrying about fine-tuning specific sentences, you should evaluate the paragraphs — as individual elements, and as parts of the whole written work.

How do you evaluate your paragraphs? Here are some things you should look for.

Organization: Is This Brick in the Right Place?

First, you should look again at the organization of the whole work. Before changing any sentences — even before looking inside individual paragraphs — you need to make sure that the order of paragraphs supports and reinforces your overall purpose. Look back at your plan.

Are the paragraphs in the order that you planned? If not, should you move them around so that they are, or do you need to change the plan?

Remember — the organizational structure is where most problems occur. Skim through, putting yourself in the reader's place. Are the major points presented in an order that will be clear to your reader? If not, now's the time to change the order by shifting paragraphs around. If you are satisfied with the order, go on to the next issue, purpose.

Purpose: Does It Help Reach my Goal?

In this step of your review, consider how well each paragraph supports your purpose. If a paragraph doesn't contribute to your purpose, fix it or eliminate it.

Fixing it means revising it so that it does support your purpose. If the main thought of the paragraph is needed, then revise the paragraph — fix it. But if you decide that the paragraph doesn't really move toward your purpose, then eliminate it. (Striking out one of your own paragraphs is not always easy, but all good writers must learn to do it.)

When you've vetted every paragraph to make sure it helps you reach your goal, you're ready to look inside each one.

Unity: Are All Sentences About the Same Topic?

Just as each paragraph should contribute to the whole work, each sentence should contribute to the paragraph it lives in. In this step, remind yourself what the purpose of the paragraph is, then read each sentence to see if it supports this purpose. And when you find one that isn't carrying its weight, decide (cold-bloodedly) whether to revise it or eliminate it.

Development: Have I Said Enough on This Point?

In reviewing for unity, your major goal was to trim fat — to get rid of (or sharpen) sentences that weren't part of the paragraph team. In reviewing for paragraph development, your job is to make sure that you have given the reader enough information — enough good sentences.

Although under-writing is not as common as over-writing, it can be a problem. It's easy to forget to include a bit of essential information — maybe a phone number, or some background information the reader doesn't have.

One way to avoid this, as we've said, is to bring another pair of eyes into play. If you can enlist a good, honest reviewer, you're likely to get a more-objective appraisal. If the reader says something like "I don't get the point here," or "this paragraph needs a little more information," say thanks, and think hard about what you can add or change to make sure you've given your reader enough good information.

Length: Should I Break It into Shorter Paragraphs?

One of the most important — and most undervalued — factors for evaluating your paragraph is its length. Again, put yourself in your reader's place.

Have you ever tried to read a book, say a lengthy novel, with page after type-filled page of long, long paragraphs? Reading it may seem like a chore.

Often, the problem is not the writing. The same work, broken into short paragraphs, with subheads, offers bite-sized chunks, with blessed white space between. It can be amazingly easier reading, a real pleasure, even though the words are almost the same. So as a favor to your readers, try to keep your paragraphs short.

Transitions: Is the Reading Smooth, or Bumpy?

Another way to help your reader is to provide transitions, bridges from one major point to the other. The reader wants paragraphs that follow each other smoothly, that flow. If the reader has to go back to the preceding paragraph to pick up the thread, it's probably because of a weak transition.

And the reader wants to have some idea of what's coming next. If you are reviewing your draft and find yourself jolted at the beginning of a paragraph, it usually means that you should insert a transitional clause or sentence, either at the beginning of the paragraph or at the end of the preceding one. But don't graft on transitions unless they're needed. If the writing flows without them, leave it alone.

First and Last Paragraphs

There's something about the way we're wired up that makes us want a clear structure in what we read. We want an opening that gets us started in the right direction, and leads us toward the major point of the writing. Then we want a middle that does the job the writer set out to do. And finally, we want closure. We want a smooth but definite windup that leaves us with a feeling of completeness.

So spend a lot of time on the first and last paragraphs. Does your opening draw your readers in and point them toward your purpose? Is it easy to read and interesting? If not, rework it. As in personal meetings, first impressions are important.

Your closing paragraph is the reader's last impression of your writing. A good ending is a smooth stop; readers should know that they have arrived at the conclusion, and should not feel a need to turn the page to find the ending. And they should know, without doubt, why you wrote it.

If you work hard at this stage, you'll wind up with clean, unified, readable paragraphs — and each one will lead your readers toward your purpose.

Summary: Points for Evaluating Your Paragraphs

- **Organization** — Arranged okay?
- **Purpose** — Does each support your purpose?
- **Unity** — Does each stick to its point?
- **Development** — Does each develop its point adequately? Include all needed information?
- **Length** — Too long, or too short?
- **Transitions** — Smooth bridges?
- **First And Last Paragraphs** — Does the first make your purpose clear? Does the last leave the reader satisfied?

— WRITING —
SENTENCES

You've stated your purpose, identified your readers, made a plan, listed points, and gotten organized. You've stated each point as a topic sentence, and drafted other sentences to form paragraphs. You've let your draft rest, then reviewed it for structure and content.

Now it's time to evaluate and improve your sentences.

Sentences flesh out the framework you've created; express your thoughts; make your writing graceful or awkward, assertive or persuasive, calming or exciting.

It's your sentences that readers will remember or forget, agree or disagree with, understand or abandon. In short, the job of your sentences is to accomplish the purpose of your writing. So they need to be good.

In this section, we'll list some of the qualities found in good sentences, make a few suggestions for developing more of those qualities in your own sentences, and point out some dangers. We'll give you some examples of sentences that work, and some that don't. We'll also touch on a few of the most important points of grammar — but we won't dwell on those.

Some Qualities of a Good Sentence

- Clarity
- Variety
- Parallelism
- Readability
- Appropriateness
- Correctness

Clarity

Your first responsibility to your reader is to provide clarity — to make your meaning clear.

Lack of clarity is not the most common sentence problem, but it's the most serious, and one of the most difficult to detect.

Ambiguity

Sometimes a sentence can be interpreted in more than one way, as in these examples:

I didn't go to the party because I thought Chris might be there. Did the writer go to the party, or not?

He was a good speaker, if not an excellent one. Is the speaker good, but not excellent? Or is he certainly good, and maybe even excellent?

I think you're asking a good price for your products. Does *good* mean fair, or too high?

The reader can't answer these questions from the sentence alone. Maybe the context — the other sentences around it — makes it clear, maybe not. As we've said, the writer knows what's meant, and may not see that it could be read another way.

Placement Problems

Sometimes the placement of words and phrases changes the writer's intended meaning.

Modifiers

We've all been taught that misplaced modifiers or dangling participles are often the culprits. And they certainly can be.

Here's one of our favorite real-world, misplaced modifiers:

The attached report is released by the engineering director with known technical deficiencies. What (or who) is technically deficient?

Now here's a dangling participle:

Rereading my draft, the problem became apparent. Who's rereading?

Prepositional phrases also need careful placement. For instance, the request for someone to "Please empty the trash cans in the kitchen" could have unintended results.

On rereading, most of us would catch sentences like these, even if we'd never heard of participles, or modifiers, or prepositions. But new ones keep sneaking into our drafts, so watch the placement of all your words and phrases, whatever names you give them.

Only *Only?*

And there's the word *only,* a dangerous little troublemaker that can wreck your sentence if it gets in the wrong place. If you say "He only promised them ten dollars," does that mean he promised them ten dollars but didn't actually pay them (as the placement suggests), or does it mean he did not promise any more than ten dollars. If it's the latter, writing "only ten dollars" would make it clearer.

Try This

Here's an "only" sentence that shows the importance of word placement. Read it through, putting the word *only* where the first asterisk is. Then read it again, shifting the *only* over to where the second asterisk is, and so on.

* He * danced * with the * woman wearing * a red scarf.

That example is fun, and it does illustrate the importance of placement. But because each sentence you write is likely to be unique, models like this one have only limited value (not "only have limited value").

It Happens to the Best

Even professional writers need editors to catch and correct such problems. Here's an example we found in a respected publication:

I was greeted by a young woman sitting at a large desk wearing a nose-ring named Rebecca.

When we come across a sentence like that, we jerk to a sudden stop. A desk wearing a nose-ring? A nose-ring named Rebecca?

But even as we chuckle, we know that we could have written something like that ourselves. How does it happen? After all, the sentence is made up of everyday words, and the structure is straightforward. But there's a problem — or two related problems.

Too Much Information

First is the awkward arrangement of the sentence parts, with *named Rebecca* hooked onto the end of *nose-ring*. But even after you recognize that problem, it's not easy to rearrange the parts in a way that will fix things. That's because of the second problem: there are just too many nouns strung together — *woman, desk, nose-ring, Rebecca.*

Do we need them all? Must we know that she was sitting at a desk? Or what her name was? If we can leave a couple of the nouns out, our repair job gets a lot easier. So couldn't we just say *I was greeted by a young woman wearing a nose-ring?* Sure, why not? (I think the writer wanted to keep the nose-ring for effect.)

Now we've fixed it. And in the rear-view mirror, it looks so easy that we wonder why the writer — or the editor or proofreader — didn't do the job. But before we pat ourselves on the back, consider this: making that specific fix doesn't buy us much, because it's almost certain that we'll never run into that exact sentence again.

Finding the Flaws

What we need is to find some way to *detect* such flaws — to recognize that there's a problem. Finding the problems in our sentences is often harder than fixing them. There's no perfect approach, but we've already touched on a couple of things that will help.

The first is to age what you write (overnight if at all possible) and reread it later, with fresher eyes. Second, and even better, have someone else read it for you. You wrote the thing, *you know* what you intended to say, and that's what you'll read. A new reader who doesn't have any history with your draft will be much more likely to catch anything that could confuse (or unwittingly amuse) your readers.

Variety

Sentence variety simply means using different lengths of sentences, and different arrangements of parts. If you vary the structure and length of the sentences you write, you're more likely to put your message across. For one thing, you'll be better able to match the structure to your intended message, and thus communicate more clearly.

In addition, your writing will be more interesting. The reader will have two payoffs: easier understanding, and greater enjoyment.

Sentence Structure

Most of our sentences consist of several parts: clauses (independent or subordinate), phrases (e.g., verb, prepositional), individual words. So we have lots of choices in how to arrange the parts to make sentences.

Still, it's easy to fall into the habit of repeating a sentence pattern, without being aware that you're doing it. Even if each sentence is okay by itself, a string of similar patterns will begin to intrude on your reader's concentration.

It's usually easy enough to mend the repetition of the same pattern. You can change the syntax (arrangement of words), maybe moving a phrase from elsewhere in the sentence to the beginning.

For instance, instead of writing

You should let your editor know if you are aware that you have a habit of repeating a sentence pattern

you could write something like

If you're aware that you tend to repeat sentence patterns, you should let your editor know this.

Sentence Length

We're not going to restate the old rule that you should always keep your sentences short. You shouldn't. Your job is to write sentences that are clear (easy for your reader to understand) and effective (they do the intended job, such as explaining, questioning, informing). You can do this with sentences of any length, if they are well written.

That said, readers don't like a string of long sentences, or of short sentences. Finding too many of either in a row can have an effect on your reader that's similar to finding a repeated word, phrase, or sentence pattern.

Let Your Computer Count

Write your draft without giving much thought to sentence length. Just concentrate on your message. When you've finished the draft, let your computer run a count for you. It'll quickly tell you the average length of your words and sentences, as well as your longest sentence.

Our computer reported that in the first draft of these last few pages, the average word length was 5 letters, average sentence length was 17 words, longest sentence was 63 words. We kept that in mind as we revised, and we asked our volunteer reader to be aware of sentence length. But we didn't change any sentences just to make them shorter, and we don't think you should either.

The best rule is to avoid strings of short or long sentences. But aside from that, if your sentences work, leave them alone.

Parallelism

Most books that give us a rule about parallelism put it something like this: *Parts of the sentence that are parallel in function should be parallel in form.*

A Brief Explanation

The *function* of a part means its job in the sentence. For example, a noun can function as a subject, object, appositive, predicate nominative, or something else.

Some of the most-common sentence parts are subject, verb, and complement. In this sentence we have one of each: *Writing requires skill.*

But we can add more. Let's go for two of each: *Writing and editing require and reward discipline and skill.*

Notice that the two subjects (*writing* and *editing*) are in the same form (both are gerunds), and so are the twin verbs and objects — one word each. Their parallel forms help us recognize them as subjects and as verbs. Now let's mess things up by changing some words so that the paired parts are not in the same form:

To write well and good editing require and give rewards for practicing discipline and high-level skills.

Now the matching parts don't match, and the sentence is a muddle. We could use grammatical terms, starting with the two subjects, and say that one is in the form of an infinitive, the other is in the form of a gerund.

Trust Your Ear

Fortunately, we rarely need to do that. Just one quick scan of a sentence like this tells us that something's wrong. So step back, reread your sentence carefully (maybe aloud). When you find the part that doesn't sound right, revise until it does. Sometimes it's easier to scrap the whole sentence and start over.

This is not to say that writers don't need to know grammar, don't need to identify parts of the sentence and the various forms they may take. Most good writers are also good grammarians. The point is that if you read and write competently, you probably don't need to analyze a flawed sentence to know what's wrong with it.

Through a process that's partly subconscious, you'll compare the sentence pattern to hundreds of thousands of sentences in your mental archives from past reading and listening. And a silent little signal will go off in your head when you come across something that doesn't conform to the rules. (The rules in your head, not necessarily those in your grammar books.) But you have to stay alert, pay attention, and keep the silent signal in good working order.

Don't Be Ruled by Rules

What you read in your grammar books and hear from your teachers are guidelines, not laws. Sometimes it's more effective to have nonparallel parts.

The man is boring, conceited, and a clod.

To make it parallel, we could change *clod* to *cloddish*. But some people would consider the original version stronger. When you feel that way about one of your sentences, leave it alone. You created it, it's yours, and you get to decide how you want to word it. Don't let rules rule you.

Readability

Readability is hard to define. Some writing can be clearly understood in one smooth, easy reading. But other writing is hard, unpleasant work, putting the reader through loop-backs, head-scratching, and displeasure.

So how do you make it easier? Here's one answer that is almost always true: the best way to make the reader's job easier is for the writer to work harder. Put another way, easy reading means hard writing.

If you follow the process we've outlined, you'll almost certainly produce writing that's more readable. Still, there will be hard work in the final stages of sniffing out sentences that stub the eye, and revising them until they don't. Here are a few specific tips for increasing readability. They will help, but you'll still have to work.

- Use the simplest, plain-English words that will get your message across. But don't be afraid to use a long word, or a technical term, when it fits your purpose and reader.

- Use the simplest sentence structures that will communicate what you want to say. You can do this and still have sentence variety.

- Try to trim any words, phrases, and sentences that are not needed. Pruning unneeded words is often one of the most effective ways to improve your drafts.

- Ask someone else — preferably someone like your intended reader — to read through your draft, simply putting a mark by anything that's hard to read, that isn't clear, or that just doesn't sound right. Then you can revise as needed.

Appropriateness

By *appropriate* we mean that the word choice, sentence structure, tone, and style fit your purpose, and that your intended readers would consider them acceptable.

All of us vary the way we talk, depending on our purpose and listeners. Your delivery of an oral report at a professional meeting will be quite different from the way you tell a joke to your closest friends. When we choose our words, we consider (consciously or not) things like formality, professionalism, tone, friendliness, attitude toward the subject and listener, and many other things. The best writers achieve good balance among these, which is to say their writing is appropriate to their readers, purpose, and subject. Again, your volunteer reader can help a lot.

Correctness

When we say that a piece of writing is *correct,* we generally mean that it conforms to rules that are widely accepted and followed by educated adult speakers and writers of our language.

Many of these rules are strictly cosmetic — they neither add to nor detract from your meaning, *in themselves.* Whether we put the period inside or outside the closing quotes isn't likely to affect our meaning.

Readers Expect Good Grammar

Still, the rules are important. Grammar gaffes can sneak into our writing, and they can hurt. Not only are they distracting, but many readers will be reluctant to trust the factual information presented by a writer who's careless with such things as grammar, punctuation, and spelling. This may not be fair, but it's fact.

Most good writers take the time and trouble to learn the rules; they also keep a trusted reference or style guide in reach, and reach for it often.

The Landa List (our own concise grammar and usage guide) will answer more than ninety percent of the questions you're likely to have when doing work-related writing. So keep it handy, and use it. And *don't* — repeat, *do not* — rely on your spellchecker and grammar checker. They'll let you down.

Your challenge is to follow the rules, but stop short of letting them push you into writing sentences that are hard to read, or unclear. If a grammatically correct sentence sounds wrong to you, it will sound wrong to your readers. Rewriting — not just correcting errors — works best.

Good-Sentence Insurance

We've said it several times, but it's worth saying once more. The best insurance of sentence quality and clarity is a careful reading of your draft by *another* competent writer. So ask for help, specifically asking your volunteer reader not only to mark errors, but also to mark any sentences that just don't sound right, or look right — for whatever reason. Then revise those sentences (and any others you notice) until they don't look funny anymore.

Getting and using the advice of a second reader is valuable not only for improving your draft, but also for improving your writing skill. The process of revising and reworking your drafts is one of the key elements in your writing-improvement program. And it's where most professional writers put much of their time and effort. Writers, like musicians and athletes, get their biggest payoff from practice, practice, practice.

—— WORDS ——

Polonius: "What do you read, my lord?"
Hamlet: "Words, words, words."

Many Words, Many Choices

Nobody knows how many words there are in the English language. We've seen estimates that range from 300,000 to 1,300,000. This abundance gives you opportunity (so many words to choose from) and a problem (so many words to choose from). In this chapter, we'll give you a few hints on your word-choice.

Three Suggestions

We'll start with three simple suggestions to help you choose words that work for you, and avoid words that work against you.

1. Think small.

Choose the shortest and simplest words *that will say what you want to say.*

Notice the italics. As we've said before, this shorter-is-better principle, like other good ideas, can be overdone. Don't be afraid to use a long word, an unusual word, or a technical term — when it's the one you need, *and* when you're sure your readers will understand it. You can even coin your own new word, if it will work for you.

2. Trust your instinct.

When you're rereading your draft, and you come across a word that sort of smells funny or looks funny or sounds funny, don't worry much about why. Just replace it with a word that's better. And if someone's doing you the favor of reading your draft, ask that person to do a little sniffing too, and to mark any word that seems odd or out of place, without having to justify it to you. Invite your reader to suggest replacements, if you like. But you're the one who'll make the final decisions.

3. Avoid overworked words.

Take *activity*, as one example among many. It's been used so repetitively and in so many different contexts that it has become almost meaningless. We hear about traffic activity, police activity, weather activity, campaign activity, construction activity, legislative activity, and lots more.

It's hard to keep overworked words out of our speech and writing, especially when we're under pressure of a deadline. But it's a goal worth working toward, and any progress will help.

Other Common Problems

The suggestions above deal with fancy words, and with overworked words. Now we'll look at some other common problems in word choice.

Unclear Meaning

A word carries meaning in at least two ways:

- *Denotation* — its definition or dictionary meaning. (You can use the d's at the beginnings of the words as a mnemonic device.)
- *Connotation* — what it suggests; an encircling cloud of additional meaning that can be at least as important as the word's denotation.

Words with similar denotations may have widely different connotations. For example, suppose a lawyer asks what a witness does for a living. The witness answers, then the lawyer restates it, saying something like "So you say that you're a writer." If we substitute another term for *say* (e.g., *claim, assert, acknowledge, admit, confess, consider,* or *would have us believe*), the meaning changes drastically, mostly because of the connotations of the words.

Be Aware of Multiple Denotations

A word's denotation can also cause problems. Here's one example. A very bright engineer referred to a written message from his supervisor as "cryptic." The message seemed clear enough to his colleague, who asked why he called it cryptic. Turns out he used the term to mean simply "short," or "concise," which could be considered complimentary. His definition is included in some good dictionaries. But there's another (and I think more common) definition: "baffling, having a hidden meaning, serving to confuse," which would not be flattering at all.

The engineer risked giving unintended offense by relying on the "correctness" of one denotation and ignoring the more commonly recognized meaning. Once again, a second reader can be a big help in detecting unwise words.

Another Example

Here's another example of a denotation problem. Suppose a technical report from a chemical lab includes these sentences: "If the temperature is too high, the reaction will occur too rapidly. We should make sure we check the speed of the reaction." Or, what if an investment manager writes something like this: "Investors should check their enthusiasm."

The problem word is *check*, which can mean "to observe, to ascertain, to evaluate," and also "to restrict, to slow down." Do we want to measure the speed of the reaction, or to slow it down? Should investors evaluate their enthusiasm, or restrict it? There's a big difference, and the writer should revise the sentence to make the meaning clear.

Connotation Confusion

Not only do some words have multiple denotations, they also have multiple connotations. *Snake* has a different and specific denotation for plumbers and herpetologists. And it also has different connotations — some scary, some insulting.

For an example of connotation-confusion, take the word *intellectual*. Suppose a politician says "I recognize that my worthy opponent is a distinguished intellectual." If we consider only the word's bald denotation, we could say that *intellectual* simply refers to someone with a good mind. But for many of us (as the politician who used the word knew), it carries a distinctly unpleasant connotation, suggesting elitism, a better-than-you attitude. Sure, lots of people use the word without intending any offense. But the outcome doesn't always match the intent, so be careful.

An Asymptotic Process

If words like *check* and *intellectual* can become booby traps, what's a writer to do? There's no simple answer. Working to improve our awareness and sensitivity to words is a lifelong job. And, to use a technical term that fits, it's asymptotic. We can keep getting closer to perfection, but can never quite reach it.

Sounds, Spelling, Appearance

Although we may not give it much thought, the sound of a word can affect a reader's attitude toward it. And even though most readers don't say the words aloud, they often subvocalize, "hearing" them silently in their heads. And what they hear will influence their reactions. Some sounds are pleasant, some neutral, some unpleasant.

Take that word *pleasant*. For most of us, it has a pleasing sound, as well as a pleasing connotation. Same with *mellifluous, expansive, sweetness,* and *lullaby.* Each one has a sound that reinforces its meaning. So together they have a sort of double-positive effect.

On the double-negative side, we have words like *yuck, slime, barf,* and *hideous.* Their sounds and meanings work together too, but this time they're reinforcing unpleasantness. A bad-cop bad-cop pairing.

Match Sound and Meaning

In both cases, the meanings and sounds are effective partners — they work together, like good teammates. But when the sound of a word and its meaning work against each other, the reader gets mixed signals that interfere with your message.

Take *ilk*, for example. Some writers use it when trying to be neutral, or even positive, as in "You English teachers and your ilk should be proud of what you've done."

Well, we may be proud of our work, but not proud to be called ilk. It sounds like a semi-polite substitute for *yuck*.

Another example is *pulchritude*. The denotation is beauty, but the sound-suggestion (a kind of connotation) is anything but. Can you imagine someone on a first date saying "I'm overwhelmed by your pulchritude"?

Summary

So in choosing your words, consider their connotation as well as their denotation, the effect of their sound, their appearance on the page, how they fit in among the words around them. These will influence your reader's response, even if the influence may be subconscious. And again, you don't have to remember all the terms we're using here. Just pay attention to the words you've used, and when you find one that doesn't seem to work, you don't have to try to figure out exactly what the problem is. Just replace the word with one that works better, and go on with your writing.

Other Words to Watch Out For

In closing out this section, we'll mention a few words and word categories that you as a writer must pay special attention to.

Confusable Pairs

One group consists of word pairs that cause confusion, even among good writers and speakers. These include *affect-effect*, *its-it's*, *regime-regimen*, and many others.

A.M./P.M.

We all know that a.m. means before noon (ante meridian), and p.m. means after noon. But what about 12:00 p.m. and 12:00 a.m.? Which is which?

It can be confusing, and possibly dangerous. If a weather forecaster says "The storm warning will be in effect from twelve p.m. today until seven a.m. tomorrow," we're not sure if the warning period begins at noon, or at midnight, and we could end up on the road at the wrong time.

The best solution is to be specific: say twelve noon, or twelve midnight.

Who/Whom

And the word *whom* is a special case. Not only is it difficult for many people to use correctly, but some readers consider it a puffed-up, pompous pronoun, used mostly by those who want to sound intelligent and sophisticated.

So should we ignore grammar rules and always use *who*? That would create one problem while trying to avoid another. But there's a middle way. You can almost always revise your sentence so you don't have to use either form of the pronoun. For example, you could change "Whom did they select?" to "Who was selected?" And sometimes you can simply leave *whom* out as in the sentence "She's the person whom they selected for the job."

This is not to say you shouldn't ever use *whom* (or *whomever*). If you like them, use them. But if you don't, you can almost always rephrase the sentence, writing your way out of the trap.

A Last Word About Words

We've looked at a tiny sampling of the huge store of words in our language. As a writer, you will work with thousands more. Words are your tools, your friends. And like other tools and friends, they require some attention. If you treat them right, they'll return the favor.

Here's a recap of what we've said about words.

- Go for simple words, when they work for you
- Don't be afraid to use long or technical words when they fit
- Keep building your vocabularies (yes, vocabular*ies* — work, personal, etc.)
- Keep a list of words that are important to you, or that give you trouble
- Keep a good dictionary in reach, and reach for it often

—— AFTERWORD ——

Congratulations. By working through this book, you have made some valuable additions to your writer's toolbox.

Of course you still have to apply the seat of your pants to the seat of your chair. But now you can sit down with a little more knowledge about what to do, and a little more confidence that you can do it.

Still, there will be times when you'll hit the writer's wall, when things sort of go blank, and you are drained and empty of inspiration.

But even when your mind seems to have shut down, something's going on up there. At some level, you're working on your problem.

So get away from the writing for a while if you can. Go do something else, maybe something active and non-intellectual. The answer may come to you suddenly, or it may come slowly. It may involve tearing up and rewriting.

The important thing is to realize that almost all writers, no matter how experienced and skilled, go through times when the writing job just doesn't seem doable. But they stick with it, or keep coming back to it, until they get it done.

You can too. To help you remember this truth, we'll leave you with one final bit of advice from a gifted and hard-working writer, one who wrote widely, wisely, and well.

> *Blot out, correct, insert, refine*
> *Enlarge, diminish, interline.*
> *Be mindful, when invention fails,*
> *to scratch your head, and bite your nails.*
> — Jonathan Swift

About the Authors

David Hatcher and Lane Goddard teach writing and speaking classes to working adults.

Their other books include

The Landa List: Grammar Guideline, Proofreading Practices, Punctuation Principles

The Dirty Thirty: Words Even Smart People Misuse

CPSIA information can be obtained
at www.ICGtesting.com
Printed in the USA
FFOW02n0731050414
4678FF

9 780972 992022